MONEY
LOVES YOU

Easy Manifestation Secrets Revealed

Blair Robertson

Aberdeenshire Publishing

PHOENIX, ARIZONA

Aberdeenshire Publishing
Box 1306
Litchfield Park, Arizona 85340

The information presented herein represents the view of the author as of the date of publication. Because of the rate with which conditions change, the author reserves the right to alter and update his opinion based on the new conditions. This is for informational purposes only. While every attempt has been made to verify the information provided in this report, neither the author nor his affiliates/partners assume any responsibility for errors, inaccuracies or omissions. Any slights of people or organizations are unintentional. If advice concerning legal or related matters is needed, the services of a fully qualified professional should be sought. Contents are not intended for use as a source of legal or accounting advice. You should be aware of any laws that govern business transactions or other business practices in your country and state. Any reference to any person or business whether living or dead is purely coincidental. All stories are true; however, some names and identifying details have been changed to protect the privacy of individuals. Hug an attorney today.

For Richard Webster

prolific author and inspirational friend

CONTENTS

Introduction

I have no idea how you found this book. Maybe you stumbled across it, maybe it was recommended by a friend, or maybe you're simply searching for something to help you change your life.

However you got here, I'm glad.

Here's the good news: You are already manifesting great change in your life. How? By reading these very words.

Money Loves You takes an entirely different approach than other books and courses on this topic of manifestation.

I'm going to help you connect with your spirit guides, who in turn will help you manifest everything that you need. We're going to focus on some taboo topics, such as the word "work," and remove a lot of the woo-woo that others teach.

I'll show you the world's easiest three-step goal setting program. I'll teach you the real secret to manifesting using the magic "fourth step" manifestation technique.

I'll teach you an incredibly easy meditation technique to help you with your manifestations.

I'll teach you my "one thing" technique that people love and have used with great success. It's easy to do and has the power to change your life.

Warning: I use the term "God" without apology. For years I've tried to be politically correct and follow the path of others by using terms such as "the universe," "the infinite," "the spirit," "the higher power," etc. But now I'm just going to use "God."

I'm not religious. I was born and raised Christian, but I walked away from all organized religion long ago. I consider myself to be very spiritual, and I choose to call the highest power God. Not the religious God. I'm talking about the creator of all.

So what qualifies me to talk about manifesting? Good question. I struggled with publishing this book because there's so much out there on this subject. But to be honest, much of the stuff that's out there is just crap. Overcomplicated, and just too much woo-woo.

I'm a spirit medium. I talk to dead people for a living. I have 30 years of experience doing that and have manifested much in my life. That, coupled with the fact that I'm the bestselling author of the book *Spirit Guides*, makes it pretty safe to say I'm pretty connected.

I've shared much of this awesome stuff at live events, and with private clients. It works. What else can I say?

This is a very short book. I don't like books that are filled with fluff. I like to get to the point as quickly as possible, and you should be able to read this in one to two hours.

That said, please don't skim it. Everyone will be different, and you'll discover that certain chapters will just speak to you. When that happens, work on that. On your next read-through, a different chapter might speak to you; work on that.

The system that I teach is deceptively simple looking, and it's tempting to skip over parts. If you want to manifest fully, master everything. It's easy, because your spirit guides will help you!

Enjoy the journey! And remember, money loves you.

Blair Robertson
Phoenix, Arizona

About Money

Money Loves You

I have good news for you: money loves you!

As you are about to see, money has no feelings whatsoever. So how can something inanimate love you?

Money is attracted to and loves those who love and appreciate it. Just like a little puppy that wants to be loved and will be faithful to whoever owns it. Money is the same.

The goal of this book is to help you understand that the more you value, appreciate, and love money, the better will be at acquiring it.

Abundance is a word that's overused today, and many of the books and teachings of other spiritual masters lead us to believe that we can just meditate and money will just appear.

It doesn't work that way. I'm going to show you how it does work. And the good news is that it's easy.

Karma

Let's talk about karma for a moment. We often hear people talk about "good karma" and "bad karma."

The truth is, there is no such thing as good or bad karma. There's just karma.

We experience karma so that we can grow. Often the best lessons that we learn in life are taught by what we would call "bad karma."

I'd like to share a mind-blowing little secret that was revealed to me by my spirit guides. It was an eye-opener for me, and I hope it is for you too.

Karma Success Secret

When we enter into this lifetime, we know in advance – before we are even born – the kinds of karmic experiences that will come our way.

Before we are born, we plan our lives out to help us learn and grow and become better spiritually.

We place those challenges into our lives knowing that we will get through them. Let me emphasize that again: we put them into our lives knowing we will get through them and win.

Here's the secret: What you perceive to be an impossible challenge is very achievable for you. And the faster you can get through that, the faster you'll succeed and the happier you'll be.

Good news! It means that what you placed before you in this lifetime karmically is a set up to win.

It's almost like going to Las Vegas and knowing that you're going to lose 30 blackjack hands, but if you hang on until the 31st, you'll win $1 million.

Karma does not guarantee that you're going to go through life smoothly. That's ridiculous. We're meant to go through bumps, turns and roadblocks to help us grow. Embrace the challenge; don't run from it.

Using that fun Vegas example, you're going to lose some of those blackjack hands. No ifs, ands, or buts. If you quit before you reach the 31st hand, you'll lose and be unhappy.

Stay, persist and have faith, and you'll win.

Now, I'm not saying go to Las Vegas and play blackjack! I'm just using that as a fun example.

Challenges are put before us to help us grow. This goes for money, jobs, relationships with a partner or family members, and more.

Karma is on your side. You just need to see it in a different light.

I've shared this story before. When my daughter was very young, she was standing by the window crying. She must been around three years old, maybe four.

"Why are you crying, Beth?" I asked.

"I want to go outside and play, Daddy, but Mom won't let me because it's raining out."

I smiled. She loves to be outside. At that moment she wasn't happy with the rain.

"You know how you love flowers so much? How we always stop and look at the flowers when we go for walks, and how much you love to smell them and pick some of them?" I asked.

"Yes."

"Well, the flowers need rainwater to drink. The flowers are very thirsty and will die if they don't get some water. You wouldn't want the flowers to die, would you?" I asked.

She stopped, paused for a moment, and then gave a huge smile as she ran off. "I like the rain, Daddy!"

See, the rain itself is neither good nor bad. It's just raining.

The karmic challenges that come your and my way are neither good nor bad. They are there just to teach us things.

And now you know the secret – that you can get through anything that comes your way – let's get moving!

Don't Worry, Be Happy

Remember the old Bobby McFerrin song, "Don't Worry, Be Happy?" That's what God wants for us.

Think about it. Isn't that the ultimate definition of happiness? To be living a life where you are happy and without worries?

Of course it is. So that's our goal: eliminate problems and build happiness. The focus of this book is financial; however, the principles apply in all areas of our lives.

You are not meant to suffer, struggle or be unhappy. That said, we've been given the gift of free will.

When we were kids we lived under the laws of our parents. When we reached the age of 18, we became adults and responsible for all things in our lives. And we have the freedom to choose what we want to do, and what we don't want to do.

Free will to choose to be happy or not

We can literally choose to be happy or not. And we can literally choose to be free of fear or to embrace it.

My goal is to help you understand you can be free of fear, embrace the future and move forward towards more happiness and attracting more good things into your life.

99% of our money problems are emotional

Almost all of our financial problems are emotion-based.

What do I mean by that?

I mean what I say: you and I have been conditioned as consumers to overspend, overindulge, and become slaves to the system.

It's not your fault

Just take a look at the word "consumer." It means to consume. The more you consume, the more you buy. Who wins there?

Add on to that the pressure to keep up with the Joneses. You can't just get by. You need to overextend yourself and buy more stuff to keep up with these other people.

Banks, credit card companies, stores, etc. are smart. They don't lend you money because they think you can pay it back quickly. They loan you money hoping that you cannot pay it back, because that earns them much more interest and profit on what they're selling.

Then the bills start coming in. And the guilt starts. And the fear.

Our problems are almost always going to be based on emotional feelings towards money.

But remember this: if you got yourself into the situation, karma tells us that you can get out. Karma tells us you can learn from this and start living fearlessly and happily.

It's not a pipe dream. It's very doable.

Money doesn't care who owns it

Money does not care who owns it. Money has absolutely no feelings. No matter how hard you try, you'll never be able to offend a dollar bill.

I recently had fun demonstrating this to a few thousand people on a Facebook live broadcast. I was talking about the topic of manifestation and the myths surrounding it. Someone joked that money didn't like them.

So I took out a dollar bill and proceeded to subject it to various tortures. I crumpled the bill up very tightly, slammed it onto my desk, pounded it hard with my palm, un-scrunched it and even poked George Washington in the eyeball!

The bill survived. In spite of being put through the mill, it came out relatively unscathed. Not only that, but it started off as a dollar and when I was finished it remained a dollar.

Money has no feelings. You cannot hurt it.

Money Loves You

How can I say "money loves you," when I just said it has no feelings? Let's examine that for a moment, shall we?

As you'll discover by the end of this book, we attract energy – both good and bad – to us according to what energy we put out.

Money doesn't care if you hate it or love it, so why not fall in love with it?

Since money has no feelings, let us focus on positive energy. Instead of thinking money is scarce, let's face the fact that it isn't.

Instead of thinking only the rich can acquire it, let's recognize it's available to us all.

And instead of cultivating false beliefs that money is evil or bad, let's give money a positive spin.

Let's give money feelings for a moment. Imagine money does have feelings. Imagine that money loves you.

Just like a puppy dog looking for a master. A puppy is only looking for someone to take care of it and love it, and in return it will bring great pleasure and faithfulness to the owner.

Money loves you. Money is in circulation for the purpose of serving. It wants to be with you.

Money was never designed to be hoarded. Money was created for compensating service.

The degree that you give and serve is the extent that you will receive.

To put it into the proper perspective, money needs you more than you need money.

Money is available to everyone. Imagine you're walking through a park and there's a $10 bill lying on the grass and nobody is around. Who does it belong to?

Seriously, pause for a moment and consider that question. Who does it belong to? Is there a name on it?

The money is available to anyone who reaches down to pick it up. The money does not care who owns it.

So why not fall in love with money, just like you would fall in love with a little lost puppy. Put away your fears of lack and decide that you're going to love money, respect money, and keep that money in circulation.

See money desiring YOU

Money loves YOU. See, money loves those who value themselves and value and appreciate it. It's like a romance. You give to it, it will return its affections to you.

Love yourself and you become attractive. When you love yourself, you radiate confidence, and that's attractive. Makes sense, right?

After all, who wants to be around a negative and depressing person? Nobody. Who wants to be around someone who is positive, confident and fun? Everyone.

You become attractive by loving yourself and acknowledging that God doesn't make mistakes. You are not a mistake. You are valuable and have value.

You become like honey, and just like bears can't resist that sweetness, money becomes attracted to you.

So decide – right now – that you love money. You value money; you value what money can do, and you would like to manifest more of it in your life. Say to yourself, "Money loves me."

No, I'm not joking. Say it. "Money loves me."

You'll probably feel a little silly saying it, but do it anyway. After all, we now know that there is an abundance of money floating around, we know that money doesn't care who owns it, we know that money can't have its feelings hurt – and we know that money can help us live happier and fuller lives.

And we deserve that, don't we?

Now, let's be clear once and for all that we are not talking about doing airy-fairy positive-thinking fluffy-thought stuff.

We are putting things in perspective – the proper perspective – and we're putting ourselves in a position to be ready for the money when it comes and happily receive it from time to time.

Your mind is like a garden. Fear and worry are like weeds, and we're going to work together to rip out those weeds in preparation for some beautiful flowers.

Now, let's get some help from our spirit guides and bring more goodness into our life. But first –

How much money is there?

There are approximately 1.5 trillion dollars in circulation at the present time.

That's a decent chunk of money. I think it's fair to say we don't need more money. PLENTY of it is around!

Spirit Guides: Your Manifesting Helpers

Who are your spirit guides?

I have good news for you. In this new journey, you will never be alone.

There is plenty of abundance to go around, and the universe is gigantic. The good news about this is that you have a spirit helper that will guide you along the way!

You have been assigned a spirit guide to help you from the moment you were born to the day you take your last breath. Everyone has at least one spirit guide; some of us have more than one.

Spirit guides are given to us by God to help us live happier, more fulfilled lives.

How do they help?

Have you ever heard the expression, "your conscience is your guide?" Well, that's your spirit guide.

And your spirit guide's job is to do its best to help get you through the trials and tribulations of life – to get you quickly to where you need to go to be happy and fulfilled.

Think of your spirit guide this way

My favorite analogy, one I love to share with my followers, is this: imagine you are driving and you come to a T in the road. You're running tight on time to get to a friend's birthday party. You don't have a GPS. You have a choice of turning left or right. If you make the wrong decision, you will be very late.

What do you do?

Well, it just so happens that there's a nice looking gentleman standing on the corner. You roll down your window and ask him how to get to your friend's place. He kindly tells you to turn right and you'll be there in just a few moments. You do, and you arrive just in time.

That's what your spirit guide is like. They don't do the work for you. You have to do the driving, and you have to follow their instructions.

Remember, as I mentioned before, we all have free will. You do not have to listen to your spirit guide. In the example above, you could've ignored the man's advice and gone in the opposite direction. Your spirit guide would not be hurt or offended.

Spirit Guides = The Key To Manifesting

Your spirit guides are the KEY component to manifesting. Your guides want and desire the very best for you. Your guides want you to be more, do more and have more.

I have written a book on spirit guides. The book is called Spirit Guides: Three Easy Steps to Connecting with Your Spirit Guides. It goes into much more detail and will be helpful for a deeper understanding. However, you'll learn enough in this book to achieve your manifesting goals.

The "catch" is that you have to work with them. Your spirit guides won't do the work for you.

There's no magic thinking here. Your spirit guides will not help you magically manifest things.

If you were to jump out of an airplane without a parachute, your spirit guides would not help you. I'm not going to ask you to embrace magical thinking. The techniques you're going to learn over the next few chapters are grounded and spiritual at the same time.

Your spirit guides want the most for you. They are on "standby" waiting to help you. Let's put them to work!

World's Easiest 3 Step Goal Setting Formula

There's a significant difference between goal setting and manifesting.

Goal setting is logic-based. In fact, I'm going to show you the world's simplest and easiest goal setting method. There's absolutely nothing to it.

Manifesting, on the other hand, is spiritual. And you can be more, do more and have more when you're tapping into the spiritual element. The differences are vast.

Setting goals is like punching a destination into your GPS and then hitting the road. You drive towards your goals.

Manifesting is something you attract to yourself. The destination comes to you! Big difference.

Again, I want to be clear that you will still have to make an effort and use the real secret – work – to manifest things. Make no mistake about that. But the differences are magical.

It makes me laugh when I hear about these expensive three-day retreats that intelligent people go on to set goals. I'm going to show you the world's easiest goal setting method.

Many years ago I used to perform as a stage hypnotist and psychic at colleges and high schools. I would attend conferences and showcase my act so these schools could book my show.

These conferences want the most bang for their buck, so they often ask performers to do a lecture. My lecture was on goal setting. And my lectures were always packed because I liked to make them fun and engaging. I called my lecture:

Blair Robertson's World's Easiest
Three-Step Goal Setting Process:

Here are the three easy steps to setting and getting any goal you wish. In fact, if you follow the three steps exactly it's almost impossible not to get your goal.

You'll see what I mean in a moment.

Step One: Decide on your specific goal.

Make it very clear, and very specific.

For example, if you want money, put down the specific amount of money you need. If you want a car, be clear on the specific car you want, including the color, make and model.

Congratulations. That was easy, wasn't it?

Step Two: Write down everything you need to do to achieve that goal.

Be specific. Break it down into simple steps that even a child could follow. After you've written down the steps, it helps to put them in numerical order.

See how easy this is?

Most people don't write down their goals. By putting your pen to paper and writing down your goals, you've already achieved much more than most of the population has.

Warning: When I share Step Three with people at live events, it usually gets a huge laugh.

Why? Because people think I'm joking. I suspect you'll probably get a chuckle out of this too, but please understand I'm dead serious.

Are you ready? Okay, I warned you!

Step Three: Do everything in step two.

That's it. No joke!

Think about it. If you do everything in Step Two, it will naturally lead you to the achievement of your goal, which is Step One.

It can hardly fail.

Most people who set goals don't make plans to achieve them. Those who do plan out their goals seldom take the action necessary to achieve the goals.

Set the goal, lay out the steps, and then take action. That's goal setting in a sentence. I just saved you tens of thousands of dollars you could have spent buying courses or flying to conferences to teach you just that.

Let's illustrate this with a fun example. You have two friends coming over tonight for dinner, and you decide you're going to make barbecue hamburgers. The problem is that your refrigerator is completely bare.

Let's examine the three steps.

Step One: Set a specific goal. That's easy; you want to barbecue hamburgers. Done.

Step Two: Make a list of everything you need to do to achieve this goal. So you take out a piece of paper and write a grocery list. You'll need buns, hamburgers, onions, ketchup, mustard, etc. You get the idea.

At this point, however, we're still dreaming/thinking about it, aren't we? We'll never reach our goal unless we take action, will we? Of course not.

So how do we virtually guarantee success? Easy, we do so by taking action. Which is why we have...

Step Three: Go to the store and get everything on that list.

Easy. Virtually fail proof, wouldn't you agree?

Now I know that that's an overly simplified example, but it's a perfect way of illustrating the three simple steps. Goal setting and achievement is not hard.

Make no mistake: you can achieve a lot with this simple three-step process. For many people, this simple process will lead to a happier and more fulfilled life.

But I'm not done with you yet. Setting goals and getting them is great. But manifesting is a whole new ballgame and can lead you to amazing levels of happiness,   joy   and   freedom.

The REAL Secret

I'm about to reveal to you the real secret to manifesting. But there's good news and bad news.

First, the bad news. You're going to have to work to get the things that you want. That's the bad news.

The good news is it's easy stuff. Easy work.

If you follow the instructions that I'm about to lay out for you in this book, you'll discover that the steps are all easy.

I once heard a great definition of the term "easy." Easy can be defined as "something you can do."

Sure, you might have to face tough challenges. You might be confronted with things that'll scare you, or daunt you, but they'll all be relatively easy.

See, there are no magic elves that are gonna work through the night to make your problems go away. No fairies are going to bring opportunities mystically to you.

The real secret is that things aren't going to happen magically by themselves; they're going to be attracted to you through your desires and your efforts.

"Work" is the magic word.

I'm of the opinion that the word "work" has been given a bad reputation. We assume that work means challenge, difficulty, sweat, and other nasty things.

As far as manifesting goes, I see "work" as simply being the effort required.

For example, my car has never taken me anywhere.

Think about it. My car is awesome, but it won't do anything until I get behind the steering wheel and put in the work/effort to drive it somewhere.

My car doesn't take me places magically. My car takes me places through my intention, work, and effort. And it's easy work!

Speaking of cars...

One of the biggest misconceptions that's been perpetuated regarding manifestation involves cars.

I'm not sure why there's such a big focus on cars; I guess it's a popular item for people to want to manifest.

I attended a conference some years ago where the manifestation leader was trying to convince people that you could think a car to appear magically in your driveway.

It's no wonder people get so depressed and think that the law of manifestation doesn't work.

I'm telling you right now: You cannot magically manifest a car to appear in your driveway. Sorry.

No matter how hard you try, how good of a person you are, no matter how strong your guides are, no matter how long you meditate... A car will not appear in your driveway.

However, with the proper intention and beliefs, coupled with that magic word "work," you really can make things happen. And yes, you really could manifest a car in that manner.

You see the difference? I'm not promoting any airy-fairy crap. The power of manifestation is real, but we also have to be real about it. We need to do OUR part.

It's not your fault

It's not your fault. Really, it's not!

Society has conditioned us to be inherently lazy. We would much rather take a pill to lose weight than hit the floor and do a bunch of push-ups.

Push-ups are free. Pills cost money. But we would rather spend the money and take the pills in the magical dream that they will mysteriously make us thin and beautiful.

Isn't that crazy? That's what society has conditioned us to believe.

I know that I'm guilty of that. I believe we all have the potential to be taken in. It's all marketing.

Frankly, the reason why so many of these manifestation courses sell so well at such high prices is that these peddlers are selling the pill instead of the work. It bothers me. It should bother you.

So I have a question for you. Are you prepared to put in the work to manifest an awesome life? If so, please read on.

If you want the magic pill, please close this book and seek out another guru. I'm not your guy.

Here's another question for you. What if I told you that doing one simple thing every single day could change your life? Would you do it?

The deal is, though, you have to do that one thing every single day. And it will change from day to day. But you have to commit to doing it.

Would you do it?

If you answered yes, you are going to love what I'm going to show you later in this book, what I call Blair Robertson's "one thing."

But there is another magic word: willingness.

When you are willing to do the work, you'll often find that you only need to do a fraction of it to achieve your goals.

Once you start going in the right direction, it's like your spirit guide starts rejoicing and cheering you on! Once in motion, they start throwing opportunities at you right, left and center.

I don't pretend to understand it. But I do know it works.

Running from challenges seems to bring more challenges, doesn't it? In contrast, running toward solutions tends to bring more solutions.

Henry Ford was once told that they could not make the V-8 motor in a single die block. The experts said so. He told them to keep working on it anyway. Their only job was to find a way to do it.

Guess what? Henry Ford discovered the single block V-8 motor.

He ran towards a solution, not away from a problem.

If you want to succeed and to manifest not only money but wonderful things in your life, then you must be willing to seize the opportunity. You must be willing to run towards the solution.

Being open to opportunity means literally being open to the unexpected. I want you to embrace expecting the unexpected.

Be open to any opportunity that comes your way – even the unplanned ones – that will advance your interests.

Think of it this way: God has at His disposal unlimited resources to get you to where you need to go. Do not limit yourself to thinking that you have to follow an A, B, C format. Don't limit yourself by your limited thinking!

Be prepared to work and accept the opportunities that come towards you. In doing so, you'll discover almost miraculous things occurring.

Don't set conditions

Here's a tip for you that I'd like you to keep in the back of your mind always...

Please don't set conditions on how things are supposed to come to you or to manifest. The more open you are to manifestation the easier it will be for the things to occur.

When you have your blinders on – so to speak – you limit how things can come into your life. That makes sense, right?

Instead, be open to the manifestations coming to you in any format. This will open up your world to opportunities you haven't thought of or considered.

Once your spirit guides know what you're looking for, they'll start drawing opportunities to you. Besides, it's more exciting and fun that way!

Money = Energy

There is no such thing as money for nothing.

Money is not going to appear magically in your bank account. Your debts are not going to vanish mysteriously. A car is not going to appear in your driveway mystically.

Money is energy. Money loves you. Money is attracted to those who invest energy in exchange for it.

Thinking about it, wishing for it, staring at a vision board, will not attract it.

Invest the energy needed, and you'll discover that it starts flowing towards you.

Let's get that energy flowing towards you!

Release Worry And Fear

Have you ever had one of those dreams where something bad is happening and you are frozen stiff?

Many of us live our lives like that: frozen because of fear and worry.

Let's address two of the biggest things that hold us back from our dreams and desires: fear and worry.

And let's address them from a spiritual perspective. Once we put fear and worry in their proper context, we are free to move forward and achieve our dreams.

> *"We become what we think about."*
> *Earl Nightingale, The Strangest Secret*

Overcoming Fear and Worry

The first and the arguably most important step is acceptance: to acknowledge where we are right now.

There's a reason why that's the first step in recovery programs.

Acceptance is powerful and profound. Acceptance is not judgmental. Acceptance is recognizing "what is" right now.

And NOW is where we need to be. Because right now is the only time that we can affect change. Right now is the only time we can begin manifesting.

You are here now. We can only work with what we have right where we stand. As the saying goes, "A journey of a thousand miles begins with a single step." Let's start here.

Where are we? Well, we are right here, right now, in what we call "today."

Today

Notice that we haven't discussed anything about money or material manifestation. If we want things to change, from bad to good, or good to great, we have to take stock of where we are at this moment.

And today is the day to do this. It doesn't matter what we've done to get us to where we are today. The past is the past. The only thing we control at this moment in time is today.

And by today I mean right now.

It is important that we get aligned with this, in the same way that a musician needs to make sure that his instrument is in tune with the rest of the band or orchestra.

I recently purchased a used guitar for a superb price. One of the strings on the guitar was not set properly, so it always sounded like it was out of tune. No matter what I would play, it would always sound off.

In other words, I was hitting the right notes, but the notes weren't in tune with the rest of the guitar, and we had a terrible sounding discord.

I took my guitar in for repair, and the technician moved the string 1/100th of an inch over. 1/100th of an inch! That small little change was all it took to put the guitar into tune.

Now it sounds beautiful.

The downside, of course, is that I can no longer blame the guitar when I play poorly!

Let's get in tune with God right now.

Yesterday

You are here now. Right here, reading this book at this moment in the living NOW.

Yesterday is gone. You don't have to continue the path that got you to here.

Forgive and forget your past mistakes, struggles, challenges and griefs.

Forgiving the past: Pain, errors and mistakes are meant to teach us and guide us, NOT define us!

It doesn't matter how you got to where you are. It makes no difference.

Maybe you made bad choices or terrible mistakes in the past.

Maybe you've overspent and racked up your credit card debt to unbelievable levels.

Maybe you've overextended yourself on car purchases or house payments.

Maybe you've let external situations bring you down to your low point.

Perhaps you're in an abusive relationship, or at least a negative relationship, and it's always bringing you down.

It doesn't matter.

I know that many people are shocked when they hear me say that, and I get it. It sounds like I don't care.

I do care. I care about you, and I want to see you do much better. But there's nothing you or I can do about the past.

Please. Answer this question honestly right now. Be brutally honest with yourself: How can you change the past?

If you're honest with yourself – and most people are – you'll recognize there's nothing you can do to change the past.

But it's human nature for people to keep pulling up the movies of the mind and re-watching and replaying all the bad choices they've made and the terrible things they've done to get where they are today.

Just watch the news. What does the news focus on? Drama. Negativity. Sad and horrible things.

Let's change that movie!

Let go of the past. It is what it is. Accept it. It's done.

There's a funny saying that goes something along the lines of, "If you find yourself in a deep hole, stop digging!"

It always makes me chuckle because it's so true. We tend to keep on digging and digging and digging, instead of just stopping to take a look at where we are.

Karma teaches us. And I admit, some lessons we are taught are hard to take.

But there really is no good and bad. Just lessons.

Karma isn't there to judge us; karma is there to teach us. You are allowed to make mistakes. You are allowed to get hurt. You are allowed to feel pain.

It's time to let go of that negativity of the past. Cut it loose and be free forever more.

Tomorrow

Tomorrow isn't here yet. Don't worry about tomorrow. Focus on faith and gratitude TODAY. We can only work with today, so let's agree to do all we can do today: no more, no less.

I once had a client who was planning an outdoor wedding and asked me if I could psychically predict if it was going to rain on that day. Unfortunately, I'm not a psychic weatherman, and I told her as much.

The woman was beside herself with worry. "If it rains it will ruin my entire day," she said.

"You have no control over the rain or the weather. Why not just simply have a backup plan that if it rains you'll hold the event indoors?" I replied.

Worry is a waste of time and energy. All we can deal with is the now.

Preparation is key, of course. If you're going to be taking a long road trip, it's wise to make sure that your tires are fully inflated, you have enough gas etc. But it's pointless to be worrying about getting a flat tire the entire time.

To be worry-free means to be living in the moment. In the example above, if you get a flat tire, deal with it at that time. So long as you prepared, there's nothing to worry about. Besides, the worry accomplishes nothing.

The woman who was planning the wedding should just have made sure there was a backup plan. If not, she was causing her own worry, stress, and grief, wasn't she?

Yesterday is gone. There's nothing that can be done about the choices we made in the past. So we need to let those go.

Tomorrow – or the future – is not here yet. Worrying about something that might happen or could happen is a waste of time.

All we are left with is today.

Love and accept yourself now

Love and accept yourself now. Not tomorrow. Not an hour from now. Now.

God and your spirit guides love you and want you to be happy and live a fulfilled life of abundance. You are not meant to be broke, scraping by or worse.

If you wish to change your material circumstances, it is unbelievably important that you be in tune with abundance, just like a musician's instrument must be in tune with the rest of the orchestra.

This is easier said than done, especially if you've been struggling for a long time.

And while it is easier said than done, don't let that hold you back. Believe and have complete faith that you were put on this earth for a purpose. Believe and have faith that you are not designed to go through life suffering. Believe and have faith that you deserve all your desires so long as they don't hurt other people.

You deserve it, don't you?

Of course you do! At the end of the chapter, I'm going to give you a meditation that will help you love yourself and value yourself more.

Good news. The moment you start loving yourself, it's like there's a transformation that occurs. You'll feel it.

You'll feel instantly better about yourself. You may even start to cry. That's okay.

But even better news is that other people will start to notice the changes in you. You can follow/do the same routine that you did yesterday, but people will notice a difference in you.

Loving and accepting yourself for where you're at not only brings peace of mind, happiness and joy, but also creates a glow about you.

People will find you more attractive and want to be around you. It's incredible, really!

But there's bad news, too. Many people don't like change. And some people react very negatively when they see other people changing for the better.

Why is that? I have no idea. Nor do I care. We aren't interested in trying to psychoanalyze others. We are interested in helping ourselves and making improvements in our lives.

That said, let me help you with a few fun ways to deal with that negativity.

How to manage external negativity

I once heard a manifestation speaker say, "The universe hates whiners and complainers."

This is completely untrue. The universe and karma don't judge. If you're a negative person, or you tend to whine a lot about things, that will be given back to you. Because you're attracting it.

Whine, bitch, moan and complain a lot, and you'll get a lot of that right back at you!

Worse, you'll attract to yourself people who LOVE that kind of thing and who will be willing to pour gas on that fire and help keep you there! Misery truly does love company.

Most people push away success and financial abundance. They do it unknowingly.

Let me say that again: the key word is unknowingly.

They've been living in limited beliefs, negative thinking, and a poverty mentality. They've been living a life of mental lack and undeservingness.

The moment you change this attitude, the moment you start loving and accepting yourself, you are opening yourself up to good things happening to you, especially in the financial areas of your life.

But those old friends, family members, and associates will start seeing changes in you. At first, it will be your attitude.

Much of the time, you'll get compliments. But when you start to change and succeed more in getting the things that your heart desires, you will start to make other people feel uncomfortable.

For the most part, this is totally natural, but unfortunately it often comes with negative comments, putdowns and judgments.

1. Let It Go

Accept the fact that you can't change others. You can only change yourself. This applies to your spouse, children, friends, and relatives. You can't change your boss or your coworkers.

You can only change yourself. So accept that. Also accept that change might make people feel uncomfortable.

Please know that their negative reactions are not your karma, but theirs. Truly, what they think of you is really not your concern, is it?

Instead of letting that bring you down, reframe it. See it as people recognizing the positive changes in you, and let that fuel your fire.

When somebody pays you a compliment, accept it, of course. Thank the person for noticing the changes.

If someone is negative to your face or behind your back, try the following technique, which I learned from Brian Tracy. It works very well.

2. Reframe the Negativity

Socrates once said that arguments die with agreement. You can use this technique and have fun with it.

Imagine a schoolyard. Bully Bobby says to Little Johnny, "You look stupid with those glasses."

Little Johnny says, "I do not!"

Bully Bobby pushes the point harder. "Do so!"

Little Johnny starts to cry. He's hurt, and Bully Bobby feels good about himself.

Let's change that. Instead of fighting, Little Johnny simply agrees and has fun with it.

Bully Bobby says, "You look stupid with those glasses."

"I sure do!"

Bully Bobby is taken aback. He pushes harder. "You are the dumbest looking dummy in the entire school!"

"Thank you!"

Bully Bobby is out of ammunition. He realizes very quickly that there's nothing that he can say or do that can "get to" Little Johnny.

Of course, Little Johnny might still be hurt, but he can have fun with it.

NOTE: It's worth pointing out that this can be an internal dialog; it need not be spoken out loud.

We are not little children, and Brian Tracy came up with a terrific technique that I learned back in the 1990s from his *"Phoenix Seminar."*

The formula is basically: "I was like that, but now I've changed."

What you are doing is agreeing with what a person is saying about your past (which is quite possibly true) and addressing the change in a positive and affirmative way.

Here are a couple of examples.

"Wow, you never enter sales contests at work."

You simply reply, "No, I never did, but I'm going for it now."

"Hey, you used to come out for drinks every single night after work and party with us. What happened?"

"I used to do that, but I need to get focused on my health and my finances now."

A coworker discovers why Emma has dropped a few pounds and sneers, "Yoga? You look good with padding; are you trying to get a man or something?"

"I was out of shape and decided to do something about it and feel great. And yes, I'd love if it gets me a man!"

You see the difference? It's a very powerful technique. It's powerful in two ways: you do not disagree with them regarding your past, and you are directly addressing the change for the better.

You're putting them on notice that yes, you have changed, and they should expect more of it.

It becomes a call of "you're either coming with me or you're going to be left behind."

Turn the negativity thrown your way – either with good intention or bad intention – and use it as fuel to spur you on to greater success and happiness.

Let's move on to Appreciation, as it goes hand in hand with acceptance.

The day that turns your life around

Motivational speaker Jim Rohn talks about the day that can turn your life around.

That's the day when you finally decide to let go of limiting beliefs, things that hold you back, things that hold you down, relationships that poison you, and you finally decide to take control of your life.

It's the day when you decide that you're going to stop being a passenger in life and take control of the steering and direction of where you want to go.

It's the day you decide that you're due to have everything you deserve in life.

If you're dead broke and up to your eyeballs in debt, today is the day you decide, "I'm done with this. This is the day I turn this around."

Or maybe you're doing okay financially, but you know there's more out there. Maybe you're one of the millions of people who are doing well but have absolutely no retirement reserves.

Today is the day you can turn that around.

Maybe you're afraid to get that new car because of what of others might say. So you've been driving a falling apart junker so that you won't stand out.

Today is the day that you can make yourself a priority. You deserve it.

It's the day you DECIDE: ***Money Loves Me.***

Will today be the day you start manifesting that foundation that will benefit people in your community, city, country, or the world?

You have a vision. Why not manifest it?

But first, you must love yourself, accept yourself and appreciate what you already have.

The moment you do so, the tides will change and return to you in great abundance.

The two-step worry buster

Here's a fabulous two-step worry buster that will help you in life. I not only teach this, but I use this in my everyday life.

There are just two simple steps. Here they are.

Step One: When you're worried, ask yourself, "Is there something I can do about this?"

If there's something that you can do, do it. Take action, and do all you can do to alleviate the worry.

Step Two: If there's nothing you can do, dump it. There's no sense worrying about something that you can't do anything about, is there?

Can it really be that simple? Yes.

Imagine you're taking your family for a picnic on the beach this coming weekend. As it gets closer, you hear that there might be a big thunderstorm. You start to worry that your day is going to be ruined.

Question: How is worrying going to change the weather? If it's going to rain, it's going to rain! There's nothing you can do about that, as it's completely out of your hands.

So we use the worry buster!

Step One: Is there something we can do about it? Well, we can't change the weather, but there are things we CAN do, so we go to Step Two: We could change our plans to another day. Or we could cancel our plans altogether. We could bring umbrellas. Or we could create a backup plan where we go somewhere else.

Problem solved. There's no sense in worrying about anything.

What about the gray areas? Traveling, for example.

I have a very good friend who worries herself sick when she has to drive a long distance. "What if I get a flat tire? What happens if my car engine dies, and I'm stuck on the side of the road?"

Obviously, there's no way of knowing when and if that'll happen.

Is there something she can do about it? Yes, she can make sure the tires are in good condition and that her engine is serviced. She can make sure that her cell phone is fully charged and that her roadside service is paid for and up-to-date. Have a spare tire and learn how to change a tire.

Other than that, there's nothing that worry's going to accomplish. Isn't that right? And given that she's done all she can do, there's no sense in worrying.

If my friend does get a flat tire, she can deal with it then in some way, can't she?

By the way, when I shared this with my friend, she laughed at how simple this technique is. She felt much better.

Try   the   two-step   method.   It   works!

Faith That You Can Manifest

Let's talk about faith for a moment.

I believe, without a shadow of a doubt, that we were never put on earth to suffer or struggle. I do agree that some of us are put into really tough positions, but I believe that these are all starting points from where we can move forward.

I have the absolute and utmost faith that we can be more, do more, and have more than we can imagine.

Money loves you. We've agreed that there's an endless supply of money floating around the world in banks and in digital form right now. Trillions of dollars. Trillions and trillions and trillions.

Money does not care who owns it. Money itself has no feelings.

Believe and have faith that you can attract into your life everything you want and need. And not just a little bit. We're talking great abundance here.

Believe and have faith that it's yours for the taking.

A powerful magic word

"Amen" is one of the most powerful and most magical words in history, in my opinion.

It's been watered down in meaning by religion and misuse – "Amen to that, brother!" – and so commonly used that most people don't realize the actual meaning of the word.

Loosely translated, "amen" means rock. It can also mean "so it is," "so shall it be," and "so mote it be."

"Amen" is a word of respect, trust, and faith in God. It follows a prayer or request and essentially says to God, "your will be done."

Here's how I look at it: don't waste God's time!

If you're going to ask God for a favor, at least do so with respect and reverence. Then, once the favor is asked, leave it in His capable hands to manifest for you in the way that He sees fit.

No matter what your religious belief is, please see the word "amen" as a powerful and effective and honorable phrase. Use it with care and good intention.

Request, don't demand

If you want to be successful at manifesting, one of the best suggestions I can give you is this: request, do not demand.

Don't be like the child at Christmastime who sends Santa a list of 20 items and then gets upset he didn't get everything he wanted.

Be open to receiving in a time and manner that God feels fitting for you.

By having faith that you will receive what you need at the times you need it, you'll live a happier and more stress-free life. You also benefit from getting the things that you like!

Ask once

Boy, is this a big one!

Because you are going directly to the source – God – you only need to ask for what you want once. Your spirit guides will take care of the rest.

You'll only cause yourself frustration by repeatedly asking for the same thing over and over again.

Don't be like a kid on a trip asking, "Are we there yet? Are we there yet? Are we there yet?" It's annoying as heck! (I know that for those of you who are parents those words are like nails on a chalkboard. I apologize!)

Many other books, courses, and gurus teach you to repeatedly ask the same thing over and over again.

It's completely unnecessary. In fact, you don't even need to go into great details when asking. Let's face it, if we are going to believe that God is the highest power of all and greatest manifester of all time, I can assure you God knows what you are thinking and what you need.

The specifics of what you're looking for are for your benefit. There's absolutely nothing wrong with meditating on your goals, thinking about them, and having faith that they will manifest. In fact, I encourage you to do so!

Just resist the temptation to pester.

I've asked for what I wanted. What now?

So here you are. You thought about what you wanted, and you were very specific about it. You have asked God to fulfill your request. Now what?

The answer is simple: take whatever steps are necessary as they come to you. Move forward with faith and gratitude for what you have and what you are about to receive.

Take your blinders off. Don't dictate or have expectations as to how things are going to turn out for you. Be open to any opportunity that comes your way, and have the faith and courage to believe that they will come.

When an opportunity comes towards you, grasp it with gratitude and thanks.

How many times have you done something for someone else and they haven't shown any gratitude? If you're like me, it's probably happened a lot. And your initial reaction is to stop giving any more.

A lack of gratitude is one of the biggest blocks to abundance.

Work: taking action with faith

Once you've given God your request, your spirit guides immediately get to work. More often than not your spirit guides will start creating opportunities for you to take action on.

Some of the opportunities will come almost instantly. Others will take a little bit of time. Either way, be open and prepared to take action and work on anything that comes your way.

Do so with faith and gratitude.

Some years ago, a friend of mine by the name of Blaine was a sales rep for an office machine company.

He needed a significant amount of money for a debt that he'd incurred. To be honest, I don't remember the exact number, but it was around $10,000.

His sales were low, and he was getting a bit dejected. He was familiar with the formula I've shared with you, as I had already shared it with him.

"This is all fine and good, but time is running out, and I don't have any new leads to follow up on," he said.

He was new to the process, so I asked him a few questions.

"Blaine, have you gone through your entire lead list and put out as many proposals as possible?"

"Yes. Every single lead on my list has been contacted," he said.

"What does your gut feeling tell you that you need to do now?" I asked.

He told me that he felt he needed to do more cold calls. I suggested that he not only do more cold calls but double the output. After all, there was nothing else to do.

If you know anything about sales or sales people in general, most of them loathe cold calling. But it's a necessary evil if you want to be in the business.

A few days later I followed up with him, and he gave me awesome news.

As a result of cold calling, he ended up picking up a couple of thousand dollars in commissions. But that's not the best part.

It gets better.

He visited one of his clients for a service call. While she didn't need anything herself, her sister-in-law worked for a major medical company in town. This pharmaceutical company had just absorbed another company and was in need of a whole fleet of business machines!

Blaine immediately went over there with his client's introduction and completed a $100,000 transaction. The commission more than exceeded his requested manifestation!

If you ask Blaine, he'll tell you money loves him! He will also tell you that the most amazing "lucky" things started to happen to him all the time. Why? Because he has faith and gratitude for everything.

Was it a fluke?

I know Blaine quite well, so I asked him if he thought the $100,000 deal was a fluke. He said emphatically NO!

He told me he learned two things. The day that he dropped in for the service call he did so unannounced. Part of his job requires him to check in on his customers from time to time. It wasn't time, but he felt compelled to drop in. Something just urged him; it was a "gut feeling," which he now credits as his spirit guides.

Did you catch that? His spirit guides caused him to pick up on an opportunity. He did, and the rest is history.

But I quizzed him a bit further. I asked him what would've happened if he had not gotten that $100,000 deal? Would that have changed anything? I mean, besides the obvious giant commission.

He told me that he realized he was lazy. He typically does very well and is one of the top salespeople at his company, but he had been "resting on his laurels" and avoiding doing cold calls.

He not only decided to go out cold calling, but he also decided to double his efforts. It was a compulsion, something he knew his spirit guides wanted him to do.

"I went cold calling with a grudge. I hate cold calling. But I listened to what you had said about being open to every opportunity. Instead of sitting on my butt and feeling sorry for myself, I went out and knocked on doors. I picked up a bunch of leads and realized, you know, it isn't so bad," Blaine told me.

The bottom line is that Blaine positively had faith in his manifestations. He had gratitude for what he had, and he was open to all opportunities.

At the risk of sounding repetitive, let me point out that he did all of the things he needed to do. There was nothing left on his to-do list. Or so he thought.

Because he was open and taking action, his service call ended up being hugely profitable. He worked. Hard.

Yes, sometimes we will need to do things that we don't like or that are uncomfortable for us. He did the cold calls. He manifested as a result of all of this.

Ask for what you want, have faith and be open to the opportunities. Be grateful for everything that comes your way, small or large.

Gratitude For Everything

Appreciation is a KEY to the power of manifesting – you must appreciate the pennies before the dollars and the dollars before the C-notes.

It sounds strange and maybe even a little bit crazy, but the moment that you accept where you are and how you got there, you can instantly appreciate where you're at.

Acceptance and appreciation go hand-in-hand.

When I split from my ex-wife, I ended up in an apartment with virtually nothing. I had a chair, a table and a bed. That was it.

At first, I was angry. More than angry. I was upset at all that I had lost, all the bad things that had been done to me, and I threw one of the biggest "pity parties" you've ever experienced. I had the oh-woe-is-me blues!

But one morning, I was walking my dog Pokie and I realized that I was free from a negative relationship, that the lawyers would work out the details of who got what, and that my life was now extremely uncluttered.

I not only accepted where I was, but I appreciated where I was. I swear to you it's the truth: I smiled from ear to ear for the first time and finally felt free.

Appreciate what you have right now. Perhaps you're in the same position that I was, with almost nothing. Embrace it. You are free from external encumbrances.

Maybe your house is in foreclosure, and the bank is trying to repossess your overpriced car that you can't afford anyway. Accept it for what it is at this moment in time, and appreciate that you are learning a hard lesson.

I didn't like the position I was in. I didn't want to be living in an apartment by myself with virtually nothing, but it forced me to look back at what I now see as a toxic relationship. It hurt, I learned, and I moved forward because of it.

You don't have to like the lesson. I certainly didn't like what happened to me!

Let me be clear, there's no requirement for you to like this process, but as soon as you embrace it, you'll ride through it faster, easier and with great rewards

The Magic
4th Manifestation Step

Do you believe in magic? I do. But not the magic that you see on television or in Las Vegas such as David Copperfield.

I believe in the magic of manifestation.

Goal setting works. But it's limited to the physical.

Manifesting is spiritual. Your guides will help you with what I call the Magic Fourth Manifestation Step.

Last year we bought a lemon tree and a lime tree. Apparently, the trees were not mature enough, so we didn't get any fruit.

This year, however, is an entirely different story. Seemingly overnight our lime tree sprouted about 200 little limes. In fact, we had so many we couldn't give them all away.

Next time you have a lemon or lime, get one of the seeds and take a good look at it. That one seed has the ability to not only sprout a tree, but from that one tree an abundance of additional fruit.

And from that abundance of fruit, an endless supply of more seeds that can create more. That seed is infinite in potential.

To me that's magic. From one tiny little seed, abundance. Have you ever considered that? Have you ever stopped to think how amazing that is?

Think about it. All that is needed is the seed, soil, a little bit of moisture, and about six hours of sunlight every day.

Of course, you'll have to plant it in a sunny spot and water it when it's dry. But really, I think you'll agree that there's not a lot of work to it, is there?

Mother Nature knows what to do with that seed.

YOU do the basic work, then leave the rest to Mother Nature.

It's the same with your manifestations. God knows what you need, and believe me, he knows what to do with that seed.

That, my friend, is the Magic Fourth Manifestation Step.

The Magic Fourth Manifestation step is simple. Give the task to God to deal with and be on your way.

Have you heard the expression "let go and let God?"

For the most part, that's what I want you to do.

Going back to the seed analogy, you are not supposed to just plant the seed and walk away. No, not at all.

Part of growing a lemon or lime tree is tending to it as necessary. You'll stick your finger in the soil to see if it's damp or dry. If it's too dry, you'll spray some water on it to keep it moist. That's your job. You need to look after it. There is work involved.

So let's change that worn-out phrase to this: "let go, let God, and help me do my part."

I believe in magic, miracles, and manifestations. Give your goals and desires to God and then do your part. Together, incredible things can take place.

The farmer and the soil

There was an old Kansas farmer who had a piece of creek bottom land that had never been developed at all. It was all rocks and brush and all messed up. He started in on it, clearing the underbrush and hauling away the rocks. Then he cultivated the soil and planted a garden, everything from vegetables on to corn. And it really became a garden spot, and he was pretty proud of what he had done.

So one Sunday morning in church after the service, he asked the preacher if he wouldn't stop by and have a look. Well, the preacher arrived, he took one look and said, "Oh, this is wonderful. These are the biggest tomatoes I've ever seen, praise the Lord. Those green beans, that squash, those melons, the Lord really has blessed this place. And look at the height of that corn! God has really been good."

And the old boy was listening to this, and he was getting more and more fidgety. And finally, he blurted out, "Reverend, I wish you could have seen it when the Lord was doing it all by himself!"

(Credit: joke told during speech by President Ronald Reagan)

2-Minute Manifestation Meditation

Let me introduce you to a powerful manifestation meditation that you can use daily to help you attract the money you love.

The word "meditation" often brings a lot of baggage with it. But you don't need to shave your head, wear weird clothing, burn incense, count beads, or chant.

Meditation is thousands of years old. I've been using it myself for 30 years and have discovered that it brings significant benefits.

I dare say that I've tried pretty much every single meditation technique you can think of, but the one I'm about to teach you now is not only the easiest, but the best, in my opinion. And almost everyone that I teach it to agrees.

Meditation brings peace of mind and grounds you and centers you in the present moment. It's the foundation on which you can build happiness and joy.

Here's why: we live in a crazy busy world. An extremely busy digital/electronic age. We are constantly bombarded – all day long – with attention-seeking messages.

Most people are missing life because their faces are glued to their so-called "smartphones."

My wife and I were recently in Mexico on a beautiful beach overlooking the ocean. There were people sunbathing by the pool, and almost every single one was on either a cell phone or another digital device.

It seems that we have been conditioned to pay more attention to how other people live their lives than to being present and living our own. Isn't that sad?

The technique I'm going to show you is incredibly simple. But don't be deceived, as that is where the beauty and magic lies.

Let me explain the technique and show you how it's done so you can give it a try. It only takes two minutes to do, and the more you practice it, the faster it will work. In fact, once you get good, this meditation technique will be just as powerful in 60 seconds.

This method has recently been made famous through the "mindfulness movement." But while mindfulness certainly deserves the credit for making it popular, this technique has been used by Buddhists for thousands of years.

Let's give it a try.

Two-Minute Manifestation Meditation

I want you to imagine right now that the air is cool enough that you can see your breath. If you were to breathe out, you would see a white cloud of air.

That cloud of air is what you're going to pay attention to.

Get yourself comfortable. You don't need to kneel, lie down, wear special clothes, or anything like that.

You can use this technique sitting, standing or doing whatever. Just get yourself into a nice comfortable position where you can remain still – comfortably – for one to two minutes.

For this example, I'm just going to assume that you are sitting down. Sitting comfortably in your chair with your feet flat and firmly on the floor, place your hands in your lap.

You're going to close your eyes, and you're going to breathe in naturally.

Do not breathe deeply. Do not try to slow down your breath. Only breathe in and out naturally.

If you have been out running, your breath is going to be very fast. Simply follow your quick breath. If you're extremely relaxed and your breath is very slow, follow your slow breath.

There is only one "trick" to doing this. When you breathe in, breathe in through your nose. When you breathe out, breathe out through your mouth.

Now, as you breathe in through your nose, imagine you can see that white cloud of air going down and filling up your lungs. Remember to breathe naturally, not deeply.

In your mind's eye, "see" that breath filling your lungs with beautiful, life-giving air.

When you need to breathe out, do so. And as you do, see that air traveling back up your throat and out your mouth.

Easily and effortlessly remain still and just follow your breath for two minutes. Shut the rest of the world off. This is your time. Know that the world will be waiting for you when you are done. You are allowed to and have full permission to take two minutes out of your day for you.

At the end of the two minutes, take a deep breath, open your eyes, and breathe out a wonderful exhale. Ahh...

Those are the basics of this super simple technique.

Now let me add a couple of nuances which makes this technique unique.

Distractions

The first time you do this, you will find that your mind is very busy with thoughts and intrusions. But there's good news: the Buddhists figured this out a long time ago.

Since you will only be doing this for a very brief time, and you know that you will be returning shortly, you simply need to train your mind to note the distractions.

Here's how you do it: Whenever a thought pops into your mind, just acknowledge it as you're breathing. Don't give it attention, just acknowledge it.

If you were speaking on the phone and a person approached you and needed to speak to you, you would likely acknowledge them by smiling or raising your finger as though to say, "I'll be with you in a moment," right?

You'll do the same here. Let's say you're meditating, and you suddenly realize you have to pick up the dry cleaning. Just keep breathing and acknowledge the thought. The thought will be there when you're done; pay no attention to it while you're meditating.

Make it fun! This is your time. It is okay for you to take one minute out of your life for you. Think about it. If you have to use the washroom, isn't it fair that you get one or two minutes of privacy to do so? So if a bathroom break is fine, so is one minute of meditation.

Your eyes

I'm often asked if you need to close your eyes when you do this. When you're beginning, I recommend that you do close your eyes. It certainly helps block off any visual distractions. That said, I routinely do this all day long with my eyes open. The cool part is that someone looking at you will simply see you as a person who is sitting, breathing, and maybe daydreaming.

Because you're not chanting and burning incense in the middle of your boardroom meeting at work, you're going to look perfectly normal. Nobody will know what you're doing. That's the beauty of this technique.

When should you do this meditation?

How often during the day should you do this? I recommend doing it every hour. It's easy to do, and you don't need anything special to do it, so there's no excuse not to.

As I mentioned, the first couple of times you do it, it will take a little bit of time to get used to. However, once you get good at it, you can do this meditation in as little as one minute with significant benefits.

You can do the meditation walking, sitting, or even in the car while you're waiting for a stoplight to change.

INSTANTLY release stress
with Blair's meditation technique

Try this. It's a great way to demonstrate quickly how powerful this technique is, and how easy it is to use.

I recently did just that on a Facebook video broadcast.

I asked the viewers to type in a number from 1 to 10 that represented their stress level, 1 being low stress, 10 being maximum stress.

Obviously, I got numbers that ranged from 1 to 10. I even had a few fun people post higher numbers, such as 11 and 12.

Then I simply guided people through the exercise I just showed you. We did it for two minutes.

Try it. Pick a number. Maybe you've had a crazy day. Pick a number that suits your stress level.

Get yourself comfortable – I recommend you close your eyes – and follow your breath. Forget about your stress number, forget about all the things that are going on in your life, just focus on your breath for two minutes.

Seriously. Stop reading. Try it right now.

Close your eyes. Breathe for two minutes.

I'll be here when you come back.

What is your new number?

Okay. Hopefully you gave that an honest try. Now let me ask you, what's your new stress number?

Whenever I demonstrate this live, or as I did in that Facebook live broadcast, most people recognize a two-to-three-number drop in their stress level.

It is not uncommon for someone to go from a stress level of eight down to five. Sometimes there are even bigger drops than that.

Why is that?

The answer is simple. When we meditate, we become one with the source: God, spirit, the universe, the higher power, or whatever you want to call the creator.

And when we are in line with spirit we are no longer alone. We are connected infinite possibilities and free from the stresses that society puts on us.

Doing this instantly re-energizes us. Meditation has so many powerful benefits that I am confident that we still don't know exactly how powerful it is. But I do know this: it is powerful, and that's all we need to know for now.

I have had many people tell me that this one technique is changing their lives for the better. That's my hope for you.

Do this every hour for one to two minutes. Set an alarm if you have to. Just do it.

Some people live and work in extremely crazy environments which make it hard to use this technique. So, get creative!

Nobody in their right mind is going to stop you from going to the bathroom for a pee break. So go to the bathroom every hour if you need to.

One of my clients is a police officer who travels with a partner. My understanding is they have to be together at all times during the day. He pretends to phone in for messages throughout the day. He is sitting right beside his partner and does a quick one-minute meditation while pretending to listen to voicemail. Isn't that a fun way to do it?

Blair Robertson's "One Thing" technique

Want to do something that will improve your life tomorrow? This is very powerful!

That sounds pretty "hypey," doesn't it? But it's not.

Here's a terrific manifestation exercise that you can do tonight. Not only is it easy to do, but it will also bring you amazing results.

Assuming you're doing your mindful meditation every hour on the hour, do this for your last meditation before bed.

Get yourself into a comfortable position and have beside you a pen and paper or digital device to record thoughts with.

Before you begin your meditation, ask your spirit guide to show you one thing that you can do tomorrow that will improve your life for the better.

Say to yourself, "Please show me one thing that I can do or take action on tomorrow that will enhance my life."

Then do your breathing exercise. In my meditation, I like to do it for a little longer before I go to sleep. I might go as long as five minutes meditating. It varies from time to time, but it's longer as I like to wind down my day this way.

As soon as I'm finished, I take a deep breath, open my eyes and let out a sigh, ahh...

Then I write down the first thing that pops into my head that I should do tomorrow to improve my life.

One thing.

Please know this: this works 95% of the time. Something will pop into your mind that you could do. It's important to understand that the task can range from something unbelievably simple to something incredibly challenging.

Either way, something will pop into your mind. Write that down and commit to doing it.

I want to be clear: you do not have to like the task that will be shown to you. But God will give you a task with the understanding that, whether you like it or not, it will improve your life.

Perhaps it will be a phone call to somebody. Perhaps it will be calling somebody to ask for forgiveness. To make a connection with somebody who you haven't spoken to in a long time. Maybe to ask your boss for a raise that you've been procrastinating about for months. Maybe to book that appointment for Overeaters Anonymous.

Do it. Promise yourself and make the commitment that you'll do it.

I have taught this technique to thousands and thousands of people, and almost without any exceptions, lives improve.

All right. Let's move forward and take a look at three easy steps to manifesting. We'll be using our mindfulness meditation technique throughout the steps.

I recommend that you work on this technique tonight before trying the next three steps.

Manifestation meditation

Every morning, do your first manifestation meditation.

Before you begin, give thanks for today. Love and appreciate yourself. Decide to embrace whatever opportunities come your way, and know that they will.

Then, do your first meditation of the day. Do so and you'll not only feel much better, but you'll be a magnet for good and prosperous opportunities.

Money Loves You. You deserve as much of it as you desire. Let's discuss how to go about doing that in a true spiritual manifesting way in the next chapter.

Putting It All Together

Spirit guides always on call

The good news is that your spirit guides are always on call. And they will help you in any area that you need help with.

Just like you need flour and chocolate chips to make chocolate chip cookies, you'll need all the ingredients to manifest your desires.

All the previous chapters were written to give you those necessary ingredients.

Remember that your spirit guides were assigned to you the moment you were born to help you get through life successfully. They desperately want to help you navigate through life and give you all the things that you desire.

Don't hesitate to ask them to help you with any areas that you may be weak in. For example, are you stressed out with worry? Then please reread the chapter on releasing worry and fear, and ask your guides to help let go.

They'll gladly assist you! You are not alone in life.

If you are stuck and don't think that there's anything left to do, ask your spirit guides, "What is just ONE thing I could do today to improve my life?"

Don't be surprised at the answer. It might not even have anything to do with your manifestations. It might be something as abstract as getting a coffee, taking a different route home, making a phone call, etc.

But know this: everything that your guides do for you is for your higher good. Everything works together. Have faith!

Don't think you deserve material things? Go to the chapter on having faith and know this: Money Loves You.

Don't try to make chocolate chip cookies without the chocolate chips! As my dad used to say, get your ducks in a row. Get everything together that you need. You're worth it!

Go for it!

If you are brand new to manifesting, there's absolutely nothing wrong with starting small. Go for it! I recommend setting a manifestation to take place within 7 to 14 days.

It could be something as simple as a nice meal out for yourself and your spouse. Or if you're single, something that you like that would be just out of your reach under normal circumstances.

If you're experienced with manifesting, I would urge you to think big. Be fearless. Set goals and have faith that they will manifest in good time. Don't hold back. You have nothing to lose, do you?

Why do I say go for it? Because when you're in tune with your spirit guides, and God, you'll resonate with your goals. You'll know the difference between a ridiculous goal versus a goal that perhaps scares you, but is achievable.

Your guides will guide you along the way. Have no fear; they are there for you.

BASIC manifestation steps

The most difficult thing I can share with you is this: there are no rules. You don't need rules. You just need to set your intentions and connect deeply with your spirit guides for success.

It's like explaining how to drive a car: there's a steering wheel to steer with, the gas pedal makes you go, and the brake makes you stop. At its core, that's how a car works, right? But you and I both know there's more to it than that.

That said, let me give you the most basic steps.

Decide on what it is you want. Be specific. Vague requests get vague responses. Specific requests get specific responses. That's Step One.

Step Two: Write out everything that you need to do and can do to achieve your desire. Break it down into steps, and be as specific as possible.

Step Three? Are you smiling right now? You should be! That's right, do everything in Step Two!

But we are not going to stop there. Because we are not going to allow ourselves to be limited by the physical. We are going to tap into the spiritual by adding the magic fourth manifestation step.

If you're religious, pray. If you are spiritual, simply give the intention to God. I happen to pray, so I simply ask God to fulfill my request, and I finish the request by saying "Amen."

As far as I'm concerned, it's done. It's in the hands of God, and if I'm meant to have what I'm requesting, it's up to God to give it to me. If not, I'm okay with it because I will learn in the process of working towards it.

Take immediate action

Whatever it is that I've requested, if there's anything that I need to do to help along the way, I take immediate action on it. And by immediate action, I mean I start the process that day.

If I need to make a phone call, I make the call. Send a message? Done. Set up an appointment for advice? I do it.

I do everything that I can to get the ball rolling. It's important to note that I don't have to do everything at once. But I don't dillydally either. If I have a list of eight things I need to do, for example, just getting the ball rolling sets in motion the manifestation process.

I live by the motto "do all you can do today, and then rest." I don't go to bed until I've done what I need to do to get the ball rolling.

Be open to EVERY opportunity

It's very important that you be open to every opportunity that comes your way. I have found meditating throughout the day keeps me mindful. Because the two-minute meditation is so easy to do, there's no excuse not to do it. I find it keeps me grounded, and spiritual.

Just as I was writing this today, I had an experience that illustrates this. My wife and I just had a barbecue island made in our backyard, and it includes a built-in barbecue. Our one-year-old standalone barbecue is still in terrific shape. We had planned to clean it up and list it for sale online.

My wife and I talked about it and felt $100 would be more than fair, cash and carry.

For fun, I set an intention that somebody in our neighborhood – or nearby – would buy it from us.

One of the contractors was in our backyard and asked my wife, Wendy, "You have two barbecues, are you keeping them both?"

"No, that one there is for sale," she said.

"Would you take $80 for it?" he asked.

Boom. Sold.

Now, I suppose you could argue that I was $20 shy of my goal.

But here's how I looked at it: it was a bit greasy and needed a light cleaning up, which would've taken me approximately half an hour to do. Maybe an hour. Then I would have had to list it, which would take about five minutes.

And then I would've had to field inquiries via email and phone calls.

We could have said no, and held out for $20, but it just didn't make sense. From my perspective, it was worth $20 to get rid of it so easily.

You get the idea. By setting the intention and being open, the opportunity came, and we took it. And we are deeply grateful for it. In fact, being the inherently lazy guy that I am, I am oozing gratitude!

Big manifestations

Is it time for a pay raise? Manifest it!

Last week I was speaking to a client of mine who felt strongly that she deserved a raise. I asked her what was holding her back.

She told me that she was afraid that her boss would not give it to her. And that's fair; it can be very scary asking for a raise. To be honest, I haven't met anybody that has felt comfortable with asking for more money. But something wasn't right here.

To make a long story short, she confessed that she wasn't sure that she fully deserved the raise just yet.

Well, that's a problem. It's important that you give before you can receive. And she admitted to me that she wasn't going the extra mile. To my surprise, she confessed that she was showing up late and clocking out early.

We dug deeper. I asked her why she was feeling that way. She responded that she didn't know. So I asked her a big question.

"What are your spirit guides saying to you about this?"

There was a long pause, and then she said, "I felt I should have been given a raise a year ago, and when it didn't come, I guess I gave up."

I asked her what she felt she should do, and what she could do right away to change the tide.

She set a goal to manifest a raise within 90 days. She committed to getting to work early so as to get back to her, as she called it, "old self."

Not even 60 days later her boss called her into the office to compliment her on her work ethic and not only gave her a raise but made it retroactive.

Amazing stuff.

I could probably share a hundred stories of people who achieved small, medium, and large manifestations. But you get the idea.

Don't get bogged down by the details. Keep it simple. Work with your spirit guides. Do your part, have faith, and manifest like crazy!

Money loves you. Aim high. And go for it!

How Do You Know That The Manifestation Is Working?

Well, the first obvious sign is that the things that you desire will manifest themselves in your life.

I know that seems obvious, but it's missed by people. Why is that? Because they often discount it as dumb luck instead of believing that it is an actual manifestation.

Be thankful and have gratitude for everything that comes into your life, even if it has nothing to do with your goal.

Your goal is not a single event. It will most likely be a sequence of small events that lead up to a big event. Be thankful for every step of the way.

You'll feel happier

One of the coolest benefits of manifestation is that you feel happier and more positive.

Why is that? Because you have let go of fear and worry. You'll no longer be living in the past. You're now living in the present.

This process causes you to grow. You'll no longer be drifting in the middle of the ocean; you'll have a destination and be eager to arrive.

Here's the best part: it happens almost instantaneously. The moment you realize that money loves you and that there are unlimited resources out there, you'll no longer be burdened by the stresses that bothered you before.

You no longer feel hindered or held back. Sure, you'll understand that it takes time to achieve your goals and manifestations, but you will be lighter and happier in the process.

You'll be luckier

Like magic, you'll start finding yourself luckier in all that you do. It will seem like you have an unfair advantage over others. And the truth is, you do!

Sales, promotions, advancements, innovations, ideas... it'll start to seem like you're always in the right place at the right time. Because you are.

Opportunities will just start presenting themselves to you. Even if you're a brand-new beginner at this, it'll happen. And as you get better at manifesting, you'll start seeing the opportunities more quickly and taking advantage of them faster.

Attract amazing people

You start attracting amazing people into your life. Positive, motivated, and influential people.

Because you'll be radiating a naturally positive attitude, like-minded people will want to be with you.

This will only be gasoline on the fire for you! Exciting times will be ahead. Their positive energy will rub off on you as yours will on them.

Negative people melt away

You'll know your manifestations are working because you'll start to repel negative people from your life. This will be uncomfortable for you at the beginning.

That said, it'll be a real blessing. When you start moving forward and enjoying successes, you'll make those people who choose to remain stagnant uncomfortable. They will likely say things to try to bring you down or curb you from your success.

You must avoid these people at all costs. It's the price you have to pay for the success you desire.

What If It's Not Working?

Just like when you're learning any new skill set, you might run into some bumps that make it appear like manifestation is not working.

This is normal. When people say to me, "Blair, I tried it, but it's not working," they are often missing something.

Let's check out a couple of these.

Too soon

Just like that lime seed example I gave you in this book, you can't plant the seed tonight and expect to wake up tomorrow to a lime tree.

Some things take time. While it is true that a lot of these manifestations will start showing signs of success immediately, often the big goal can take a bit of time.

Start focusing and showing gratitude for each opportunity and sign. Keep the faith and know that things will turn out well in good time.

Unrealistic goals

Some people try to manifest unrealistic goals.

If you are living in a tent, running from debt collectors, and have not paid child support in years, it's unreasonable to set a goal that you'll be a multimillionaire in a year.

You must crawl before you can walk, walk before you can run.

And let me be clear. Nothing is stopping you from being a millionaire or even a multimillionaire – eventually.

Set goals that stretch you, not break you.

Unclear goals

The biggest mistake most people make with manifesting is that they are unclear in what they want.

Be specific. "I need money" is not specific.

"I need $5,000 by April 1 to pay for XYZ" is specific.

Your spirit guides need something specific to work with. Your spirit guides are useless with the first example, but can make a lot happen with the second one.

Not the Right Time

Sometimes it's just not the right time.

Do you give a child everything they demand when they demand it? Of course not.

That shouldn't dishearten you. Not manifesting something in your timeframe is not a sign that God doesn't want you to have it or that you don't deserve it. It just means you don't have it yet.

Be careful of being tempted to give up. Or quit. Or say something silly like, "this manifestation stuff doesn't work." That, to God, is like a child having a fit because she didn't get her way.

Instead, ask you Spirit Guides for guidance.

Not Doing Your Part

Of course, the biggest reason for manifesting not working is the seemingly most obvious: you haven't done your part. I would urge you to re-read this book and make sure you are doing all you can do on your end. You must drive the car if you want to get to your destination.

Conclusion

I'm excited for you. I really am. I'm excited because you now have the tools to manifest your dreams.

Money loves you. It really does.

Use the tools in this book. Use whatever tools you need: you can use them all or just the ones you need.

But please use them.

You were not put on earth to struggle or suffer. So drop that notion and start living abundantly. Live abundantly for you, your family and the causes that you love.

Believe and have faith that your Spirit Guides are there to help you and that God wants the best for you. Do your part and let the abundance come.

Love and light to you.

Blair Robertson

About The Author

Blair Robertson is a world-renowned psychic medium dedicated to demonstrating that love never dies, and that God is all around us. Based in Phoenix, Arizona, he lives with his wife Wendy, the love of his life.

Blair has been featured on the Discovery Channel, Fox News, NBC, ABC, and hundreds of radio shows worldwide. He has produced a number of CDs, DVDs, and free online seminars on spiritual subjects.

Blair Robertson tours widely, giving demonstrations of communication with the afterlife. He was once branded a "comedium" by one of his fans for his sense of humor and compassion. Blair excels in delivering messages of love in a loving way.

He has a weekly inspirational newsletter, and we invite you to visit and subscribe at http://www.BlairRobertson.com

Check out Blair's latest books by visiting Amazon or wherever quality books are sold.

Made in the USA
Monee, IL
13 September 2021

77917110R00061